CW00343437

SOCIAL STUDIES ESSENTIA

REFERENCE MATERIALS

Liz Brown

MEDIA ENHANCED BOOKS

AV2 BY WEIGL™

ADDED VALUE • AUDIO VISUAL

www.av2books.com

Go to www.av2books.com, and enter this book's unique code.

BOOK CODE

AVP36992

AV² by Weigl brings you media enhanced books that support active learning.

AV² provides enriched content that supplements and complements this book. Weigl's AV² books strive to create inspired learning and engage young minds in a total learning experience.

Your AV² Media Enhanced books come alive with...

Audio
Listen to sections of the book read aloud.

Video
Watch informative video clips.

Embedded Weblinks
Gain additional information for research.

Try This!
Complete activities and hands-on experiments.

Key Words
Study vocabulary, and complete a matching word activity.

Quizzes
Test your knowledge.

Slideshow
View images and captions, and prepare a presentation.

... and much, much more!

Published by AV² by Weigl
350 5th Avenue, 59th Floor
New York, NY 10118
Website: www.av2books.com

Copyright © 2020 AV² by Weigl
All rights reserved. No part of this publication may be reproduced, stored in a retrieval system, or transmitted in any form or by any means, electronic, mechanical, photocopying, recording, or otherwise, without the prior written permission of the publisher.

Library of Congress Control Number: 2019937708

ISBN 978-1-7911-0886-1 (hardcover)
ISBN 978-1-7911-0887-8 (softcover)
ISBN 978-1-7911-0888-5 (multi-user eBook)
ISBN 978-1-7911-0889-2 (single-user eBook)

Printed in Guangzhou, China
1 2 3 4 5 6 7 8 9 0   23 22 21 20 19

032019
103118

Project Coordinator: Heather Kissock   Designer: Ana María Vidal

Every reasonable effort has been made to trace ownership and to obtain permission to reprint copyright material. The publishers would be pleased to have any errors or omissions brought to their attention so that they may be corrected in subsequent printings.

Weigl acknowledges iStock, Getty Images, Shutterstock, and Alamy as its primary image suppliers for this title.

Table of Contents

What are Reference Materials?

Reference materials are sources of information that can be used to gather content for essays and school projects. There are many types of reference materials, such as encyclopedias, almanacs, atlases, newspapers and magazines, and websites.

What reference materials do you have in your house or classroom? Have you used them for a school project?

Noah Webster worked on *An American Dictionary of the English Language* for **22 years**.

The first encyclopedia had **37 volumes**. It was published in Ancient Rome in the year 77 by Pliny the Elder.

The first English **dictionary** was published in 1604. It contained approximately **3,000** words.

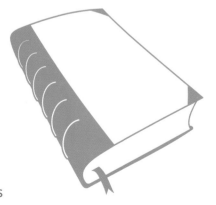

Reference Hunt

Find an encyclopedia, almanac, atlas, and newspaper. Visit a website that might be useful for a school project. Examine each of these items, and make a chart on a piece of paper. On one side, write the types of reference materials you have examined. On the other side, write a sentence about how you think these resources would be useful for school assignments.

A newspaper and an encyclopedia are useful tools for gathering information about world events. After looking at these materials, can you list some of the similarities and differences between them?

What are Tables of Contents and Indexes?

Many reference materials have a table of contents and an index. These tools help the reader find information quickly. The table of contents is at the beginning of a book. It lists the book's chapters, or sections, and the page numbers where they begin. The table of contents lists items in the order that they appear in the book.

An index is an alphabetical list of names and subjects that are included in the book. Beside each index entry, there is a list of page numbers where the subject can be found. Indexes are usually located at the back of a book.

Do your schoolbooks have a table of contents? Do they have an index?

SOCIAL STUDIES ESSENTIAL SKILLS

Using an Index

Read the following text about the Cherokee Native Americans, and select a topic, such as arrow points, that you would like to learn more about. Then, find a book about Native Americans at the library. Use the index of the book to find more information about the topic that you have selected.

*The Cherokee peoples used many tools to hunt and fight wars. The bow and arrow were important tools for the Cherokee. They were used to hunt large animals, such as deer. To make arrow points, the Cherokee sharpened pieces of bone, chipped flint, or stone. The same method was used to make spearheads, tomahawks, axes, and hammers. To make these tools, the Cherokee used stones to sharpen and grind a groove around the edge of a bone or a rock. They tied a strip of **rawhide** to the groove to use as a handle. This stopped the tool from slipping out of their hands.*

The Encyclopedia

An encyclopedia is a book or an electronic collection of articles that cover all fields of knowledge. These articles are usually arranged alphabetically according to subject. Some encyclopedias have so much information that they take up many volumes, or books.

There are two types of encyclopedias. One type is a subject encyclopedia. Subject encyclopedias only include information about one field of knowledge. An example of a subject encyclopedia is one that deals with medicine or law. A national encyclopedia includes information about one nation, or country.

Locate an encyclopedia online or in the library. Find an article on a topic that you are interested in, and read it.

Is there other information you would you like to know about the topic? Check other encyclopedias to see what they include.

The other type is a general encyclopedia. General encyclopedias contain basic information about many different topics. One volume of a general encyclopedia might include facts about snakes, soda, and San Francisco.

Abraham Ortelius created the first **atlas**. It contained **70** maps and was published between **1570** and **1612**.

The **oldest** newspaper in the United States is the *Hartford Courant*. It was first published in 1764 and is still published today.

Writing an Encyclopedia Article

Read the following **biography** about President Obama. It is written like an encyclopedia article. Encyclopedia articles give a summary of the most important information about a topic. Write an encyclopedia article about yourself. Think about what others would want to know about you if they were looking for details about your life. Include important information such as your birthday, where you live, and some eventful times in your life.

Barack Hussein Obama II was born on August 4, 1961, in Honolulu, Hawai'i. He was the 44th president of the United States. Obama graduated with honors from Harvard Law School in 1991. He married Michelle Robinson in 1992. They have two daughters, Malia and Sasha. Obama served as a U.S. senator from Illinois from 2005 to 2008. In 2006, he wrote a book called The Audacity of Hope: Thoughts on Reclaiming the American Dream. *It became a national best seller. Obama became the first African American president of the United States, and served two terms beginning in 2009. Obama is known for signing many landmark bills into law during his presidency, including the Affordable Care Act.*

The Almanac

An almanac is a reference book that is published each year. Like an encyclopedia, an almanac can have information on many different topics. Some almanacs contain information in one specific area of knowledge.

Almanacs contain up-to-date **statistics** and lists, often in the form of **tables** of information. These books are useful for accessing up-to-date information, such as the population of a country and important events from a specific year.

Almanacs are usually organized by general topics such as science, business, entertainment, sports, and the world. Information also can be found using the index.

Almanacs contain information about landmarks and cities. Find a general almanac at your library. Use it to get the population size of the state capitals of the United States. Then, find the national capitals of other countries in the world. Can you tell by looking at this picture what country this is and what the name of the capital city is?

Learning about the World

Using an almanac, research information about another country in the world. Find out the country's population, **birth rate**, and size. Look up other statistics that you think are interesting. Report your findings to a friend or classmate. The example below contains information about Mexico.

Report on Mexico

*Mexico's population in 2018 was 125,959,205. The birth rate per 1,000 people is 18.1. Forty-nine percent of Mexico's population are male, and 51 percent are female. Ninety percent of the population of Mexico can read and write, and 23 percent of the population between the ages of 25 and 35 have a college degree. The country covers an area of 761,606 square miles (1,972,550 square kilometers). The **population density** is 165 people per square mile (64 people per square kilometer).*

The Atlas

An atlas is a collection of maps bound together as a book. There are many different types of maps in an atlas. Maps can show information such as geographic, **social**, **economic**, and historical data.

In an atlas, you can find continents, countries, cities, and towns. To locate a city, look up the name of that city in the atlas index. The index will always have the page number for maps that show where the city is located. The city's location on the map is shown using coordinates, or intersecting lines of **latitude** and **longitude**.

Using an atlas, find a map that contains the city or town where you live. To find your city or town, search through the index. The coordinates of your city or town will be located in the index. Turn to the page where your city or town is shown, then trace a line with your fingers along the lines of the latitude and longitude coordinates. The point where your fingers meet should be the place on the map where your city or town is located.

Map Quest

Below are the latitude and longitude coordinates for a well-known city in the United States. Find its location on the map, and identify the name of the city and the state where it is located.

Latitude: 40° 49' North

Longitude: 73° 57' West

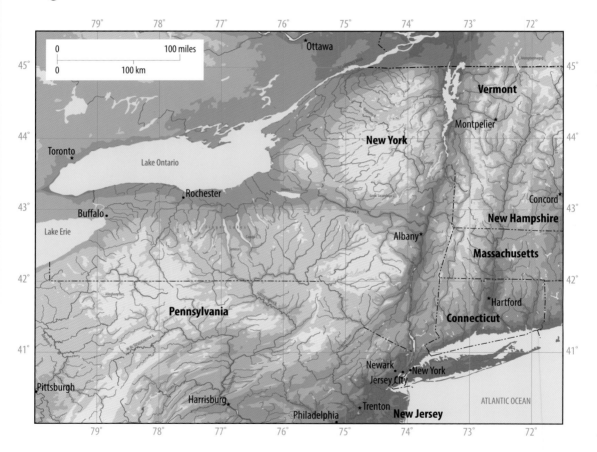

Answer: New York, New York

Newspapers and Magazines

Newspapers and news magazines are useful sources of information. If the publications are recent or new, they will contain information about current events. If they are older, they can be helpful as a **primary source** for historic research.

Some magazines and newspapers are **archived**, or stored, on electronic databases. Using **search engines**, you can sort through past issues for information about a topic.

Read today's newspaper or an article in a recently published news magazine. Share what you learned in the article with a friend.

The Constitution in the News

Learning about the **Constitution** is an important part of social studies. Even though the Constitution was written in 1787, it still plays an important role in the lives of United States citizens. Often, there are articles in current newspapers and magazines about the Constitution.

Visit your library and find recent copies of *Time* magazine and the *USA Today* newspaper. Find an article that talks about the Constitution. What is the constitutional issue that is discussed? How does it impact your life?

Websites

Websites provide a quick and easy way to find information needed to complete a project. However, not all of the information on the internet is accurate. It is important to verify that the information provided on a website is correct. Credible sources include academic institutes, official organizations, and government sites.

Useful websites can be found using search engines. Using search operators, which are symbols, and words effectively can help improve the results of a search. Here is a list of some common search operators that can be used in many search engines.

"OR"	*Put "OR" between two search terms to search for either of the two terms.*
"AND"	*Use the "AND" between search terms to look only for websites that contain both of the terms.*
" "	*Place quotation marks " " around a search term to look for the whole word or phrase.*

Testing Search Operators

To test how search operators work, start with a widely used search engine such as Google. Try searching for information about the Constitution using only that word. Then, try adding other words to your search. Use the article below for some ideas for other words to use. Use the operators "OR" and "AND." Do you get different results? How are the search results different?

The Constitution was created at the 1787 Constitutional Convention in Philadelphia, Pennsylvania. Delegates from the 13 states worked together to create a unified government. Edmund Randolph, the governor of Virginia, proposed the Virginia Plan. This plan was to create a national government with three branches. The branches were the executive, legislative, and judicial. Randolph thought that this plan would help the 13 states work together more easily. Some delegates did not like the Virginia Plan. All of the delegates worked together to reach a **compromise**. The Constitution outlined the new plan and how the new government would work. The Constitution was finished on September 12, 1787.

Evaluating Sources

When using reference materials for research, it is important to ensure that the materials are current, reliable, and accurate. To determine if the information you are gathering is current, check the publication date on the inside cover of the book. Reliable website articles often have a publication date as well.

The list of questions that follows will help you determine if a source is current, reliable, and accurate. Some questions are better for websites, while others are more suitable for books.

Does the information have an author?

Does the author have contact information listed so you can contact him or her if you have questions?

Does the author list sources that he or she used to write the information on the site? Is there a bibliography, or a list of works cited, in the book?

Is the source free from spelling or grammatical errors?

Is the website affiliated with a school, library, government, or other organization?

Does the website contain links to other reliable sites?

Has the website been updated recently?

If you answer yes to all of these questions, your source is probably reliable and good.

Reliability Test

Read the following paragraph. Do you think it was written by a reliable source? How can you tell?

The Lincoln Memorial

*The Lincoln Memorial is located in Washington, DC. This national memorial honors Abraham Lincoln, the 16th president of the United States. He governed the United States between 1861 and 1865, during the time of the Civil War. Lincoln fought to keep the United States together. He also worked to ensure that all people living in the United States had equal rights and freedoms. After Lincoln was **assassinated**, U.S. citizens decided to build a monument to honor him. Construction began on February 12, 1914. Carvers, designers, and painters worked on the memorial for eight years.*

From the outside, the Lincoln Memorial looks like a Greek temple. It has 36 columns, or pillars. The columns represent the number of states in the union when Lincoln died. A large statue of Abraham Lincoln sits between the columns. The statue is a reminder of the importance of freedom and unity.

Written by Professor June Cleaver at the University of American History on June 25, 2007.

Plagiarism

Copying another person's work and submitting it as one's own is called plagiarism. Often, people do not mean to plagiarize. Accidental plagiarizing happens when people do not properly cite, or credit, the sources they used in their research. Sources are usually cited in text and at the end of a paper in the bibliography.

To keep from plagiarizing when writing a paper or putting together a project, do not copy information word for word from your sources. Instead, paraphrase the author's ideas. Paraphrasing is putting another person's ideas into your own words.

Two of the most common methods for citing sources in a research project are the Modern Language Association (MLA) style and the American Psychological Association (APA) style. Each of these methods has a style guide that shows students how to properly cite information from different sources.

Paraphrasing

Practice paraphrasing by reading a passage of text, and then, without looking at it, write down the main ideas. The following text is about Navajo Native Americans. Read the information, then paraphrase its main ideas on a piece of paper.

It is difficult to imagine that people lived in the United States nearly 1,000 years ago. The Navajo first settled in the southwestern United States between 1200 and 1500. The Navajo traveled to the United States from Canada. They moved from place to place around the Southwest, hunting animals and gathering food.

The Navajo first encountered the Spanish and the Mexicans in the 17th century. The Navajo received horses, goats, and sheep from the Spanish. The Mexicans taught the Navajo silversmithing. The Pueblo shared their weaving and pottery-making techniques. These skills changed the Navajo's ways of life and became very important to their economy. Over time, the Navajo also became shepherds and farmers.

Today, the Navajo are one of the largest Native American tribes in the United States. More than sixty clans, or families, of Navajo live in Arizona, Colorado, New Mexico, and Utah.

Putting Your Knowledge To Use

Knowing when and how to use reference materials is an important skill. Test what you have learned by answering the following questions.

1. **Where are indexes in books usually located?**

2. **What is an encyclopedia?**

3. **What is the purpose of an atlas?**

4. **What does putting an "OR" between two search terms in a search engine do?**

5. **What is paraphrasing?**

Answers:

1. Indexes are usually located at the back of a book.

2. An encyclopedia is a book or an electronic collection of articles that covers many fields of knowledge or just one subject.

3. An atlas is used for looking up geographical locations and data.

4. The search engine looks for either of the two terms.

5. Paraphrasing is taking an author's ideas and putting them in your own words.